HANDFULS

OF

PURPOSE

By

Mrs. Charles E. Cowman

COWMAN PUBLICATIONS, INC.

Los Angeles 38, California

Printed and Bound by Rand McNally & Co.

To

His Ambassadors Who

Are Girdling the

Globe

Whose Fellowship Have Made

Glad the Years

Foreword

THE BIRTHPLACE of books is often discovered in out of the way and obscure places. Readers seem always interested in hearing of the circumstances under which such books are born.

Following many years of intensive service, we came to a sudden bend in the road and were bidden to enter a school on the back side of the desert—God's training school for His soldiers.

In Way's translation of 2 Corinthians 10:4-6, we read, "*We do not fight with merely human weapons . . .*" No! The weapons with which I war are not weapons of mere flesh and blood, but in the strength of the Lord they are mighty enough to raze all of the strongholds of our foes. I can batter down the bulwarks of human reason; I can scale every fortress that towers up bidding defiance to the true knowledge of God. I can make each rebel purpose my prisoner of war and bow it into submission to the Messiah.

In the year 1373 Julian of Norwich wrote: "He said not thou shalt not be tempted; thou shalt not be afflicted, but He did say, thou shalt not be overcome." We are to rise unvanquished after every blow—we are to laugh the laugh of faith, not fear.

To preserve the fruits of a triumph one must help his fellow-warriors to gain a similar conquest. The strong, muscular limbs of a soldier are retained by sharing his blood with the entire army.

For this cause STREAMS IN THE DESERT was born. Its lessons shared have resulted in a fellowship with many thousands scattered over earth's vast domain.

Among this number were found a multitude whose hearts and homes had been windswept with sorrow. For these a special ministry was necessary. CONSOLATION went to comfort those who mourn.

In the year of 1938 a companion volume for STREAMS was born. Another book of daily devotions—SPRINGS IN THE VALLEY.

David prayed, *"When I am old and grayheaded, forsake me not until I have shown thy strength to this generation."* A youth leader walked into my office one morning and said, "Give us a book for the youth of our generation." MOUNTAIN TRAILWAYS FOR YOUTH was the answer to that urgent request.

Another interim of time passed. Letters poured in from those in their eventide of life. Many felt caught in the web of discouragement—others felt unwanted. To this vast company, TRAVELING TOWARD SUNRISE presents a reminder of God's unfailing promise, *"Even to your old age I am He. I have made, I will bear. Yea I will carry you."*

Long had the year of 1955 been talked of as a memorial year. Joshua 14:10. It is altogether fitting that HANDFULS OF PURPOSE should be the answer to the latest surprise requests.

Bookmaking is not my calling. The volumes already mentioned came along while engaged in the calling to which my life has been committed.

> Tell all the world there is sight for its blindness,
> Balm for its healing, songs for its dumb.
> Blood for its cleansing, hope for its dying,
> Tell them of Jesus, and bid them to come.

HANDFULS OF PURPOSE is the God-given portion to His handmaiden while following by the side of the reapers of rich golden grain out in the vast whitened harvest fields of the world.

This crowns my task!

September 1955   MRS. CHARLES E. COWMAN

I could not do the work the reapers did,
Or bind the golden sheaves that thickly fell;
But I could follow by the Master's side,
Watching the marred face I loved so well.
Right in my pathway lay many a ripened ear,
Which I would stoop and gather joyfully;
I did not know the Master placed them there,
Handfuls of purpose that He left for me.

CONTENTS

HANDFULS
OF
PURPOSE

| Chapter One | **MARTYRS OF MONOTONY** |

IN A SMALL CHAPEL at a midwestern university there is a small painting of two hands raised in prayer. As you look at it, the picture seems very simple, but it tells a fascinating and inspiring tale that reaches back to the year 1490.

In France two young woodcarving apprentices had often confided in each other their desire to study painting. However, such study required a far greater supply of money than they possessed, for Hans and Albrecht were practically destitute. Finally, they hit upon a solution—let one work and earn money while the other studied, then when the fortunate one became rich and famous he would in turn help the other.

While Albrecht went to Venice, Hans sweated away as a blacksmith. As quickly as he received his wages, he would send them on to his friend. The weeks stretched into months, the months into years, and at last Albrecht returned home to his native land—an extraordinary master—a rich and renowned painter. Now it was his turn to help Hans. The two men met in joyous reunion, but when Albrecht looked at his friend, his eyes filled with tears as he discovered the full extent of Hans' sacrifice. The years of hard and heavy labor had calloused and bruised his friend's sensitive hands. His fingers would never be able to handle a painter's brush.

In humble gratitude, that distinguished artist, Albrecht Durer, painted a portrait of the work-ridden hands that had toiled so that he might develop his talent—he captured the full significance of the words of Jesus in Luke 24:40, "*He showed them His hands.*"

In the Talmud there is a story of a peasant worker who fell in love with the daughter of his wealthy employer. She returned his love and, despite her father's violent objections, married him. Aware of her husband's ardent love for learning, she insisted that he go to the great rabbinical academy at Jerusalem to slake his intellectual thirst. He studied for twelve years while she, disowned by her family, suffered in poverty and loneliness. Though still eager for advanced studies, he returned home. When he reached the door of his house, he overheard his wife saying to a neighbor that even though the pain of separation seemed more than she could bear, she hoped and prayed that he would return to the academy for further study.

Without a word to anyone, he went back to the school for twelve years more of study. Once again he turned determined footsteps toward his native village, but this time all Palestine was singing his praises as the most brilliant and scholarly mind of his generation. As he entered the market place, he was caught in the crowd of a reception committee that had gathered to honor their native son. While people were pressing about him, he saw a woman— her body bent, her face wrinkled—desperately trying to break through to reach him. Suddenly he realized that this prematurely old woman, whom the milling crowd ignored and pushed back, was his beloved wife.

"Let her through," he shouted. "Let her through. It is she, not I, whom you should honor—she who sacrificed while I studied. Had it not been for her willingness to work and wait, to serve and suffer, I would be today a peasant laborer and not Rabbi Akeba."

During my many years of missionary service, it has been my privilege to cross the ocean a number of times. The great ocean liners of this day provide incomparable speed and steadiness both in stormy and calm seas. One of the great thrills of the trip is the experience of descending to the engine room and watching the massive engines as they throb, throb, throb in their unresting motion, night and day, never ceasing until port is reached. Away down in the hold of the vessel, far below waterline, are engineers and firemen. These dedicated seamen stand by their engines and boilers hour after hour. The only reward for their vigilance is the steady and rhythmic operation of the powerful engines that are so vital to the life and progress of the ship.

During the entire trip these workers are hidden away out of sight doing their duty and working untiringly at their ordinary, commonplace tasks. They would not dare to say while out in mid-ocean, "What we are doing is so monotonous, let's give up this uninteresting work!" No! None would dare to suggest such a thing. These faithful workers are indispensable to their captain and their company. The trip could not possibly be made without their own bit of individual service.

When after a number of days land is sighted, not only can the captain and the deck officers and sailors say, "We are bringing her safely into port." Ah, no! It required the hidden-away service of the men far out of sight. It took the captain and the entire crew to bring the ship safely in.

Today we find ourselves conditioned only for the spectacular. We scan our newspaper only for momentous news—our admiration is so linked with the glamorous that we have almost forgotten the usual every-day activities of the average person. We have been so busy acclaiming and applauding the amazing exploits of our military technicians, the extraordinary maneuvers of national and world statesmen as they direct the destinies of great masses of people, and the miraculous discoveries and contributions of scientific geniuses and industrial giants that we have failed to appreciate those individuals and accomplishments which have played and presented their vital roles in the drama of life—toiling quietly but effectively behind the scenes, performing only so-called minor parts.

We remember Moses, the great emancipator, law-giver, prophet and leader; we forget Aaron, his brother, who served as his spokesman before Pharaoh.

We remember Joseph, the fair-haired dreamer who rose to fame and fortune on Pharaoh's throne and brought deliverance to his famine-ridden family; we forget Reuben and Judah and the other brothers who watched over their father and the entire household of Israel and brought them safely to Egypt.

We remember Abraham, the courageous founder of a new faith; we forget his wife, Sarah, who as his companion and co-worker, also sacrificed and suffered.

We remember Ruth; we forget Naomi.

We remember David; we forget Jonathan.

Yes, those who fashion the extraordinary, who perform the spectacular and who achieve the glamorous necessarily stand on the pinnacle of the world's admiration and acclaim; however, we must never forget to be everlastingly grateful to those who slave at the bottom. It is well to remember that nothing spectacular will ever be achieved without the devoted toil and dependable performance of those whose daily tasks seem drab and undramatic. Let it always be remembered that the most amazing achievement of our time—the splitting of the atom—was not the accomplishment of just a few scientists, but also of thousands upon thousands of ordinary men and women working in obscurity, working without any knowledge of the ultimate goal that was being sought, working without any expectation of reward, but working, working, working.

Some years ago a lady approached me at the close of a meeting with the following words, "I wish that God had called me to the mission field! I live such a useless, monotonous life, just spending my days in humdrum work that seemingly amounts to so little." Further conversation brought to light the fact that she was a faithful worker in her church, and her influence in the community had inspired many to abundant living and fruitful service.

A life need not be great to be beautiful. There may be as much beauty in a tiny flower as in a majestic tree, in a little gem as in a great jewel. A life may be very lovely and yet be insignificant in the world's eyes. A beautiful life is one that fulfills its mission in this world, that is what God made it to be, and does what God made it to do. Those with only commonplace gifts are in danger of thinking that they cannot live a beautiful life—cannot be a blessing in this world. But the smallest life that fills its place well is far lovelier in God's sight than the largest and most splendidly gifted—yet fails in its divine mission.

> "Far better in its place the lowliest bird
>   Should sing aright to Him the lowliest song,
>   Than that a seraph strayed should take the word
>   And sing His glory wrong."

Chapter	AFTER ALL,
Two	THERE IS
	GOD!

GENERAL SIR W. EDMUND IRONSIDE tells a remarkable story of how Haile Selassie on one occasion rebuked him for his lack of faith. It was during the Italian occupation of Ethiopia and the Emperor was living in exile in England. The General was talking to Haile Selassie regarding the tragic circumstances surrounding his dethronement. He said, "Your Majesty, what are you going to do now?"

The Emperor looked into the face of the General and calmly replied, "After all, there is God!"

Our world of today is completely engulfed in an atmosphere of suspicion, distrust and fear. These are the obvious by-products of a generation locked in the seemingly inescapable embrace of an octopus-like monster

23

called war, whose deadly tentacles reach out and fasten themselves onto people of every land and climate. All would seem lost if we were to judge things humanly, but, "After all, there is God." There are times in history when it is necessary to reiterate great Bible truths; to learn that the Infinite comes to the aid of the finite. When man's resources come to an end, God's possibilities begin and we find the glory of the impossible.

How great is our God? How much do we believe in Him? Is He to us a living, bright reality, or is He a God far off in the heavens who is deaf to the cry of His needy children?

Indeed not!

It is wonderful to know that we can be sure of God—sure of His presence when we are called to go through tremendous tests of faith, when in the pathway of His purposes and plans He permits us to go through twisting storms and howling tempests. Faith is validated and glows brighter when mighty storms rage without.

In the days of the invincible Spanish Armada, England faced sure defeat. The tyrannical Spanish monarch had vowed, "I am going to wipe that nation off the face of the earth." His great Armada stood poised for attack. It was a dark hour indeed—but, "After all, there is God!" Lightning flashed, waves rose and fell with increasing ferocity until the mighty fleet was dashed into kindling wood. England's dark night gave birth to the glorious sunrise of God's loving intervention.

Napoleon Bonaparte swore by all Heaven that he would completely subjugate all the forces of the world. He assembled a mighty army. Christians stood fast and prayed. God's rain began to fall in torrents, and instead of his being able to attack as he had planned at six o'clock at Waterloo, he could not launch his attack until late morning. The delay resulted in the "Little Corporal's" defeat, and the cause of righteousness and freedom was upheld.

Again, Napoleon started for Moscow with a half-million picked soldiers of France. Carnage and havoc threatened the very foundations of the world. All of a sudden a snowflake kissed Napoleon's cheek. He laughed and brushed it off. A dozen snowflakes fell. Napoleon laughed again, but not so loudly. The velocity of the storm increased until there was a regular avalanche of snowflakes. The men and horses plunged and floundered in the deepening drifts until a half-million French soldiers lay frozen on the steppes of Russia.

The French leader had once said: "God is on the side of the heaviest battalions." He was right; he just forgot that God stables His battalions in the sky.

In May and early June of 1940, 335,000 men were trapped on the sands of Dunkirk. It looked as though they would be wiped from the face of the earth. German land, air and naval fire beat the shores with merciless intensity and precision. They were surrounded and all that was left was a little sandy beach. It did not seem that all the powers of earth and heaven could ever rescue these men. Death seemed certain, but God sent a fog. The fog became thicker and thicker, and it lay over the evacuation area like a dense blanket until all the men were saved.

"After all, there is God!" He has His sun. He has the snow. He has the fog. He is the master of every circumstance. *"The Lord hath His way in the whirlwind and storm."* Nahum 1:3.

The stress of these days is producing in God's children an unwavering faith. The poor, weak faith of Christians is being fanned into a burning flame, and we are pressed into knowing no helper but God. David, the Psalmist, left us this testimony: *"We went through water but thou broughtest us out into a wealthy place!"* That place was God himself. Finding Him and His boundless resources, we have all.

Yes, it would certainly take the sting from many a goading trial if we could see, even as Job did, no hand but the divine. He saw God's hand behind the gleaming swords of the Sabians. He saw God's hand behind the lightning flash. He saw God giving wings to the careening tempest, and he saw it in the awful silence of his rifled home when there was nothing left. *"The Lord gave, and the Lord hath taken away,"* was his testimony, and he added a note of praise, saying, *"Blessed be the name of the Lord."*

Job's faith reached its climax when, seated

upon his bed of ashes, he could say, *"Though he slay me, yet will I trust him."*

When our faith is tested to the breaking point, let us look up and trust, and we will have the same testimony that the beloved Christian ruler of Ethiopia has—"After all, there is God!"

Chapter	**FEAR**
Three	**NOT**

THE JUDEAN HILLS had long given of themselves unselfishly to the grazing flocks of the
faithful shepherds from nearby Bethlehem,
but now, they were to perform a new role.
Here was the stage-setting for the greatest
music and the most important announcement
ever heard by human ears.

*"And there were in the same country shep-
herds abiding in the fields, keeping watch over
their flocks by night. And, lo, the angel of the
Lord came upon them, and the glory of the
Lord shone round about them: and they were
sore afraid. And the angel said unto them,
Fear not: for behold, I bring you good tidings
of great joy, which shall be to all people. For
unto you is born this day in the city of David
a Saviour, which is Christ the Lord."*

How startled those shepherds must have

been when the very heavens opened and the strains of angel chorus echoed and re-echoed through the quiet hills and vales! Little wonder that they trembled at this unusual happening and were "sore afraid." How tender and assuring must have been the voice that bade them, *"Fear not: for behold I bring you good tidings of great joy."*

Dr. Courtland Meyers draws this interesting illustration and comparison: "The two words, 'Fear not' are the *thrush-notes* of the Bible! The thrush sings in the depths of the forest; a bit of music like that which occurs nowhere else in the bird world. It is marvelously sweet! It is unique and absolutely alone. There is nothing else like it. Man's genius has many times tried to capture it within the bars of music, and always failed in the attempt. It seems almost as if this note was dropped out of the angel's music. Maybe they left it in the world the night they sang at Bethlehem."

Yes, "Fear not" is a part of the angelic chorus, but is it a part of every day life? Surely, it would apply to every situation and to all conditions—it must be a certainty—a positive reality. The sweet strains "Fear not" apply as much to our twentieth century life as they did to the calm pastoral life of Judea!

Biography affords a wonderful stimulus to faith. Let us seek to find how those in other generations, in other decades, weathered the storms of life.

Consider the story of Shadrach, Meshack and Abednego. Their refusal to bow down before the pagan god of Nebuchadnezzar so infuriated him that his very sanity was threatened. Roughly they were dragged into his fearsome presence, but there was about them a calmness and a serenity that could only be understood in the light of their answer to the great monarch: *"If it be so our God whom we serve is able to deliver us from the burning fiery furnace, and he will deliver us out of thine hand, O King. But if not, be it known unto thee, O King, that we will not serve thy gods, nor worship the golden image which thou hast set up."* Then, as later in the great cremation oven, they were aware of an unseen Presence—fear was completely dissipated.

A contemporary illustration of this fear dispelling Presence was attested to by Mr. F. S. Smythe as he related the experiences surrounding his lone attempt to climb Mt. Everest. "All the time that I was climbing alone I had a strong feeling that I was accompanied by a second person. This feeling was so strong that it completely eliminated all loneliness I might otherwise have felt. It even seemed that I was tied to my 'companion' by a rope, and that if I slipped 'he' would hold me. I remember constantly glancing back over my shoulder, and once, when after reaching my highest point, I stopped to try to eat some mint cake, I carefully divided it and turned around with one half in my hand. It was almost a shock to find no one to whom to give it. It seemed to me that this 'presence' was a strong, helpful and friendly one, and it was not until Camp Six was sighted that the link connecting me, as it seemed at the time, to the beyond, was snapped, and, although Shipton and the camp were but a few yards away, I suddenly felt alone."

Returning now to Biblical illustration, it is interesting to note that every portrayal of Daniel, as he stood amidst the lions in the dark, subterranean den, pictures him with an expression of absolute calmness. He knew there was no need for fear—he was under the protection of Almighty God.

As we read the Psalms, we find that David did not always live in green pastures and beside still waters. He met conflicts and had battles to fight. But, listen to his testimony, *"I sought the Lord, and He heard me, and delivered me from all my fears."* What a marvelous deliverance! He found that fear was a deadly enemy. His fears held him in a dungeon. Even the *"noonday was as darkness about him,"* and there was no song in his heart, but the light broke upon his soul and burst through the gate that led him into joy and liberty. What a testimony he left when he came down to the close of his life's little day!— for under God's low-bending sky, under God's stars of everlasting promise, in God's own companionship, he just went to sleep. *"Yea, though I walk through the valley of the shadow of death, I will fear no evil: for Thou art with me!"*

Look at Stephan as he marched to a martyr's

death. How calmly he went, and, "*all who looked upon him saw his face as if it had been the face of an angel*." What a triumph of faith and deliverance from fear!

I have always admired the triumphant spirit of that great man of God, Saint Paul. He was in the midst of life's greatest calamity; in a place where the angry waters determined to swallow him up. He held onto that splintered old spar as it tossed on the stormy Adriatic Sea and said to his fellow-travelers, "*Fear not! I have a message from God! An angel has appeared and spoken these words to me: Fear not, Paul! Not one of you shall perish.*"

I once heard the famous Scottish preacher, John McNeil, relate this personal incident. During his boyhood in Scotland, he worked a long distance from home. The walk home took him through a dense forest and across a wide ravine. The ravine was known to house such nefarious tenants as wild animals and robber gangs. Darkness would often gather before he got to the woods, and he said, "How I dreaded to make the last part of the trip! I never went through those woods without trembling with fear.

"One night it was especially dark, but I was aware that something or someone was moving stealthily toward me. I was sure it was a robber. A voice called out, and its eerie tone struck my heart cold with fear. I thought I was finished. Then came a second call, and this time I could hear the voice saying, 'John, is that you?' It was my father's voice. He had known my fear of the ravine and the darkness of the forest, and he had come out to meet me. My father took hold of my hand and put his arm around me; I never had a sweeter walk in my life. His coming changed the whole trip."

That is God's relationship to you and me! He is your Father and my Father. Through the darkness and mist we hear His voice—He has come to meet us. Just at the time we need Him, He will be there. Through the darkest moment of life our Heavenly Father says, "FEAR NOT! Here is My hand! I will walk the rest of the way with you."

That is Christianity—that is faith! *"Fear thou not."*

| *Chapter* | **DIVINE** |
| *Four* | **RESOURCES** |

OUR WORLD is one of vivid contrasts and fluent extremes.

What a contrast there is between the arid, lifeless, barren desert and the luxuriant oasis with its waving palms and its glorious verdure; between gaunt and hungry flocks and the herds that lie down in green pastures and beside the restful waters; between the viewless monotony of the shimmering plains and the mountain heights, resplendent in magnificent beauty.

What a difference there is between the aridity of an artificial, stinted existence—a desert existence—and the almost over-powering fruitfulness of a rich fertile valley, washed by gentle rains and bathed in filtered sunlight—the abundant life!

This lesson of contrasts finds its daily counterpart in the lives and experiences of Christian people. There are some who seem always to be kept alive on scant measure. Their spiritual garments are threadbare. Their existence is as barren and fruitless as the desert wastes. Life seems to have dried up, and purpose has so dehydrated that they wander aimlessly around the margins of life.

There are others who daily experience the inner peace and happiness that comes through a vigorous faith in the Saviour—a practical day-by-day faith that insures victory and "life more abundant." In a word, this is an experience that reaches out into the infinite as well as the eternal—sailing on the shoreless and fathomless seas of God and His unlimited grace. It is a life guaranteed to gratify the parched and arid soul. *"They shall be abundantly satisfied with the fatness of thy house,"* was the testimony of the Psalmist.

Do you ask, "How shall I find this more abundant life?"

At Calvary!

Our precious Saviour, by His death on the cross, proclaims "liberty to the captives" once and for all.

"Some years ago," wrote a friend of mine, "I was speeding across our great country in a train. One day in the quietness of the almost deserted car I found myself reading the first chapter of Acts. I was thinking of 'the higher life'—the 'abundant life,' of which, just then, we had heard a great deal. I was vexed and almost angry at the little headway that I was making. All at once my eyes fell upon the words, *'But ye shall RECEIVE power. . . .'* The word RECEIVE gripped me. This was something very different. This was not climbing up, but the coming down of something, and it was the thing I needed. This was not a thing wrought out of me by agony and effort, but something put into me like a seed in the earth. 'Receive,' I said, ashamed, and with my difficulties silenced, 'of course I can receive. That needs no genius, no goodness, but only want. Any beggar can take a coin if it be given to him.'"

"Ye shall receive"—think carefully about these words until they kindle expectation and the boldness that claims it as your own. Ye shall RECEIVE. How vast a difference it makes!—the reception of new life; partakers of a new nature—the divine nature.

In the ditch there grows a briar, scratching, tearing. It sighs within itself and says, "Ah me, I cannot think what I was made for. I have no beauty and no worth. If only I were a bunch of violets on the bank, I might make somebody happy—but a briar! If I were but the oak tree whose branches come out so far and whose leaves make such sweet music as they rustle under the prodding of gentle breezes—then I would be of some good."

But now, here comes the gardener and digs up the briar by the roots and plants it in his garden. The briar is heard to mutter, "He doesn't know me or he wouldn't waste his time like this. He will never get any good out of me—a wretched briar covered with prickers!" But the gardener just laughs and says, "If I cannot get any good out of you, maybe I can put some good into you. We shall see."

Now, however, the briar was sadder than before. "It was bad enough living in the ditch, but to be among all of the sweet and dainty flowers and still be just a briar is just terrible.

I knew I could never amount to anything!"

One day the gardener came and made a little slit, put a tiny bud in it and fastened it there. After a few weeks the little briar-rose was aflame with color, and its fragrance was most exquisite. What a transformation! There was now little resemblance to the scraggly, bedraggled briar whose first home was in the ditch.

Our Heavenly Father is the husbandman. He understands the rough stock of our humanity. He knows its evil nature and its little worth, but He also knows how to put within it a new nature. Not of our struggling or strife does it come, for it is not from within that this grace must spring, but by our surrender to the divine Gardener—letting Him have His Way perfectly with us in everything. If we will but permit Him to put into us what He desires, He can get out of us what He wills. Receiving is more than asking—it is claiming and taking. The manifestation of His indwelling may be as gradual as the development of the bud in the briar, but be assured that it will be there.

Look again at the words, "*Ye shall receive*

power." This means infinitely more than the parable of the briar indicates. It is not only the reception of a germ of new life that is promised; it is a change of soil, of atmosphere, of condition. We are told that the shivering weeds of the Arctic regions are nothing less than our forest trees—the stately oak and the sturdy elm. The very grasses and ferns of the temperate climate become trees in the tropics.

Who knows of what development we are capable when we find ourselves lifted from the dreary realm of our coldness and doubt to dwell in the summer of God's presence. How often have men and women without special genius or great gifts risen up into resistless power for God by the indwelling might of His Spirit!

If God can paint the blush on the bud which hangs from the limb of the rose, and make the dew-drops of morning tremble like molten diamonds on the virgin-white lip of the lily; if He can plant the rivers in lines of rippling silver, and can cover His valley floor with carpets of softest green, tacked down with lovely daisies and laughing daffodils; if He can scoop out the basin of the seven seas and pile up the rugged granite of the mountains until they pierce the turquoise skies; if He can send a Niagara thundering on a mighty and majestic minstrelsy from century to century; if He can fuel and refuel the red-throated furnace of a million suns to blaze His universe with light; if on the lovely looms of heaven, He can weave the delicate tapestry of a rainbow, and at eventide fashion a fleece of crimson to curtain the couch of the dying sun, and across the black bosom of the night that follows bind a glittering girdle spangled with ten thousand stellar jewels; then we cannot doubt His willingness to provide for us, His children, fathomless oceans of spiritual power which are ours "to receive" as we walk daily in glad obedience to His voice. The power of God through His Spirit will work within us to the degree that we permit it.

The choice is ours.

| Chapter | STIRRED |
| Five | NESTS |

A TENSE DRAMA was being enacted in the lofty crags of the desolate mountain heights. A little eaglet perched precariously on the edge of the nest. He weaved with uncertainty from one side to the other in frantic indecision—he wanted to leave the familiar shelter of the nest and soar into the unexplored expanses, but the small, needle-sharp talons only dug in deeper as he looked down. It was too much. He looked with terrified eyes up toward his mother as she circled overhead, but even as he watched, the mother eagle plummeted toward the nest and struck it with such violence that it disintegrated and the little one was plunged into the great spaces.

He was flying! The mother eagle swooped low, and as she circled him she called to let him know that she was there right beside him—her tireless wings would give support if it was needed.

Suddenly the eaglet looked down. His flight was instantly interrupted by a paralyzing terror that robbed him of his strength. His wings flapped wildly at first, but so great was his fear that he just gave up and stopped trying. The little bird dropped like a stone toward the uneven cliffs sprawled below.

Like a flash the old mother eagle shot under him. He landed with a thud and his quivering talons dug in deeply as he tried with frenzied effort to gain his balance. The two soared as one for a few moments. Suddenly the mother plunged headlong into the depths below, leaving the little one momentarily suspended in space. This time, however, his wings flapped with confidence and the descent was completed with the glad assurance of a job well done. The only trace of the momentous struggle was a handful of feathers floating earthward that had been painfully torn from the mother eagle's back as she made her last valiant effort to plant confidence in the feathered breast of her little one.

I am sure that the ancient and very wise author of Deuteronomy 32:11 had viewed a similar scene as he wrote: "*As an eagle stirreth up her nest . . .*"

God, like the eagle, stirs our nest. Yesterday it was the place for us; today there is a new plan. He wrecks the nest, although he knows it is very dear to us. He loves us too much not to spoil our meager contentment. He knows that our nests of complacency and self-satisfaction must be disturbed if we are to ever explore life's high altitudes. Our devotion to comfort and the currentless ease of yielding listlessly to the status quo so deadens our sensitivities that we lose sight of God and His purposes for our lives in Christ Jesus.

The eaglet says, "Teach me to fly!" Christians often sit idly by wishing they were more like their Lord. Unfortunately, neither is likely to recognize that their prayer is answered when their nest is toppled over!

No, the very nature of the eagle compels him to early desert the sheltered nest and conquer the limitless heavens. He is the king of birds; he must soar high.

47

Fellow Christians, the writer of the book of Isaiah likens us to these great masters of the skies: *"They that wait upon the Lord shall renew their strength; they shall mount up with wings as eagles. . . ."* Our heritage through the matchless love and sacrifice on Calvary of the Saviour provides for all of God's children the capacity to live in the stratospheres of life in complete harmony with His will and purpose. The Spirit-filled life is *the winged life;* the unsurrendered life clings with uncertainty to the nest.

Our wonderful Saviour, by His death, proclaims "liberty to the captives." We are set free; not to take refuge in an easy-going and powerless faith, but to grow spiritually into virile "sons of God"—well able, with His help to withstand the temptations that defeat. Using again the example of the eagle—the way is not always easy, but the storms of life strengthen our ability to soar above them into the infinite calm of God's presence.

Look at the eagle as he sits on the crag and watches the sky filling with blackness—the forked lightning piercing the eerie depths.

There he sits perfectly still, turning one eye and then the other toward the coming storm. But he never moves until he begins to feel the burst of the breeze and knows that the hurricane has struck him. With a scream he swings his breast to the storm, and uses its fury to lift him up into the heights. He is borne up upon it, and that is what God wants of every one of us, His children!—to "mount up on wings as eagles!"—to turn the storm clouds into chariots.

Beloved, we will never get anywhere by looking at the dark side of things. A friend of mine once made this interesting statement: "My religious organs have been ailing for a long time ... but I got out my wings, and have taken a change of air." That is just it—we forget our wings! We travel along our roads as mere pedestrians, and we are sorely overcome—for the hostility of our circumstances weary us to the dust. In a hundred different ways we can be cribbed, cabined and confined—and our religious organs are in danger of becoming diseased; of losing their brightness, both in mood and discernment. We have kept too close to the road and have not responded to the upward calling.

Yes, as our unreserved commitment is made to a waiting and ever-loving Heavenly Father, the power of the *winged life* is ours, and we rise from our prisons or from our tiresome road into the high heaven of spiritual rest and vision. The higher we soar the more clearly we are able to discern the will and purpose of God.

One day I observed a prairie eagle mortally wounded by a rifle shot. His eyes still gleamed like two circles of light. Then he slowly turned his head and gave one more searching and longing look at the sky. He had often swept those starry spaces with his powerful wings. The beautiful sky was his home—it was his domain. A thousand times he had exploited there his splendid strength. In those far away heights he had played with the lightnings and had raced with the winds. Now, so far away from home, he lay dying because he forgot and flew too low.

God has called us to victory and attainment. He knows no failure. His home is in the heav-

ens. He earnestly desires that we have the
strength to "mount up" and assume our right-
ful place.

> I am an eagle
>   born to fly
> Up the stellar highways
>   of the sky.
> Along the milky way
>   where blazes
> New dawns, new planets,
>   new days.
> I am man-born, God-led,
>   sky-bent.
> Almost omnipotent.

William Stidger

| Chapter Six | ARE YOU LOOKING UP? |

SEVERAL YEARS AGO while visiting certain of the Northern European countries, it was necessary for me to cross the North Sea in a large ocean liner. During the first days of the voyage we sped along over calm seas, but suddenly we were overtaken by a frightening tempest. The waves were like great mountains, and we were lifted to their heights. The great ship rocked and rolled, creaked and groaned. The faces of the passengers were blanched white with fear. Even the little ones clung to their mothers, sensing the nearness of danger—the very air was surcharged by an ominous foreboding of impending destruction. When it seemed that surely the ship had endured to the very limit, a man appeared on the scene. There was no trace of anxiety or concern on his face.

His presence radiated calmness, rest and peace. With a voice full of gentleness he assured us, "all's well," and our fears disappeared.

Who was that man? The captain. He had taken that vessel through many a long voyage, plowed rough seas, met terrible storms, and had always arrived safely into port—flags of victory flying at top mast.

What have we to fear? Why do we look down? Where now is thy God? Is not our Captain on board, and with one word can He not say to the waves and winds, "Peace be still," and they obey Him? With hushed hearts let us listen for His sweet whisper of assurance, "All's well. It is I; be not afraid." With Christ in the vessel we smile at the storm.

Faith is not a fair-weather product; it grows amid storms. It inspires us to keep our sights raised above the rolling waves of life.

A steeplejack was once asked how he kept from falling when he was climbing a high chimney or steeple. "Surely the ground must seem a great distance away as you look down," it was suggested. "I do not look down," he replied. "If ever I should look down to the ground, I would lose my nerve. I always look up, then I am safe."

Yes, one whose faith is continually stimulated by *the upward look* gives no ground to the attempted encroachment of discouragement, melancholy and despair, for these are arch-enemies of faith. No matter how great the trouble or how dark the outlook, a quick lifting of the heart to God in a moment of real, actual faith in Him will completely alter any situation and turn the darkness of midnight into a glorious sunrise. Take away faith, and in vain we call to God. There is no other road betwixt our souls and Heaven. Blockade that road and we cannot communicate with the Great King. Faith links us with Divinity.

Madam Guyon, while shut up within prison walls, wrote the following: "Give no place to despondency. This is a dangerous temptation, a refined, not a gross temptation of the adversary. Melancholy counteracts and withers the heart and renders it unfit to receive the impressions of Grace. It magnifies and gives a false coloring to objects, and thus renders your burdens too heavy to bear."

"Why go I mourning because of the oppression of the enemy, while they say daily unto me, where is thy God?" An outstanding minister said that one evening he found himself staggering along under a load that was heavy enough to crush half a dozen strong men. Out of sheer exhaustion he put it down and took a good look at it. He found that it was all borrowed. Part of it belonged to the following day; part of it belonged to the following week, and here he was borrowing it that it might crush him *now*—a very stupid but a very ancient blunder.

Never yield to gloomy anticipations. Who told you that the night would never end in day? Who told you that the winter of your discontent should proceed from frost to frost, from snow and ice and hail to deeper snow? Do you not know that day follows night, that flood comes after the ebb, that spring and summer succeed winter? Place your hope and confidence in God. He has no record of failure.

"Though an host should encamp against me, my heart shall not fear; though war should rise against me, in this will I be confident. Why

art thou cast down, oh my soul? Hope then in God for I shall yet praise Him."

There's a white morning light on the hills; the stars shine through the cypress trees. Lift up your heads, fellow Christians, our God is the master at earth's console.

| Chapter Seven | **HOPE REVIVED** |

DAY AFTER DAY, PIERRE, an infamous Parisian beggar, stood on his chosen corner and whined coins from passers-by who were generous only because of their eagerness to be rid of the repulsive derelict.

The studio of a well-known artist was situated just a few feet from Pierre's station, and throughout each day the artist could be seen watching the beggar with unconcealed fascination. The day came when he could no longer resist the urge to paint Pierre's picture. He moved his easel and canvas to a position near the window and began to paint feverishly.

When the painting was finished to his satisfaction, he stepped to the window, rapped to attract Pierre's attention and motioned to him to enter through the front door. Without a word the artist stationed him in front of the covered easel. With a flick of his wrist the drape fell to the floor and exposed the finished work.

"Who is it?" Pierre asked in wonderment.

Slowly a gasp of recognition hissed through his lips, "Can it be me?" he cried incredulously.

"That is the beggar, Pierre, as I see him," replied the artist.

"If that is the man you see, that is the man I will be," was Pierre's classic retort.

Our Bible portrays vividly the arrest of a woman taken in the act of adultery. She was brought to the temple for trial and sentence. As she stood before the tender Master of Galilee, He looked deep into her restless eyes and saw a broken, battered and bruised woman. That long look of the Master penetrated deep —He saw a guilt-sick soul crying for the peace that comes through faith in a living Saviour.

Jesus looked from one of her accusers to another until under that steady gaze each had felt the guilt of his own insidious existence and had slipped furtively away without further accusation.

The awesome silence was broken by the low voice of Jesus, "Neither do I condemn thee. Go and sin no more."

These simple words of the Master framed the Magna Carta for her life. She was set free from the bonds of sin that had held her prisoner—she could now hold her head high and move among her neighbors without shame.

How wonderfully kind and courteous our God is! He did not belittle the outcast woman. He did not remind her of her sinful past and condemn her. No indeed! With all of the tenderness that Jesus could muster, He spoke words that brought hope to her troubled heart.

Recall with me the words in John 1:42, *"And he brought him to Jesus. And when he beheld him, he said, Thou art Simon, the son of Jona: thou shalt be called Cephas, which is by interpretation, a stone."*

Jesus knows us with infinite and awful accuracy. He knows our hearts, and He says, "Thou art . . . " If this were all, what tragic hopelessness would defeat us! In the same breath, and separated only by the briefest pause, Jesus hastens to add, "Thou shalt be . . ." Simon, the self-sufficient man became Peter, the rock-man of Pentecost. It is ours, too, to share gladly with Him as He fashions our future. Remember, He has not only said, "Thou art," but also, "Thou shalt be."

A great and majestic cathedral was the focal point of interest in an ancient city. Among other things, it was noted for a very special stained glass window. Its fame became so great that people came from far and near to gaze upon the splendor of this masterpiece of art.

One day a very violent storm swept across the land, and the great window was jolted loose and crashed to the marble floor below. It seemed hopelessly shattered into thousands of unidentifiable pieces. The people were crushed by this catastrophy that had so suddenly bereft the town of its proudest work of art.

They sadly gathered up the broken pieces, piled them in an old box and carried them down into the cold, damp church cellar. Some time later, a stranger appeared at the church door and asked to see the beautiful window. They told him of its fate. He asked what they had done with the fragments, and they took him to the cellar and showed him the broken pieces.

"Would you mind giving these to me?" asked the stranger.

"Take them along," was the reply, "They are no longer of any use to us."

Months later an invitation reached the custodians of the old cathedral. A famous artist announced the completion of his greatest work—a stained glass window. At the appointed moment, the master-artist ushered his visitors into the presence of one of the most exquisite works of art their eyes had ever beheld. They gazed entranced upon its rich tints, its wondrous pattern and cunning workmanship.

The heavy silence was quietly broken by the low voice of the artist. He said, "This window has been made from the fragments of your shattered one. You may take it back with you and return it to your cathedral."

> He came to mend earth's broken things,
>   That Carpenter of old:
> God's broken law; men's broken hearts;
>   And broken dreams untold.
> He came to mend earth's broken things,
>   To rest each weary soul;
> His body broken on the cross—
>   Broken, to make us whole.

One Sunday morning the congregation of a large city church became restless with ill-concealed consternation. Their favorite soprano soloist was scheduled to sing, and she had never failed them—until now. What had happened? Where were her parents? Their pew was empty, too!

Bonnie's friends waited in breathless anticipation. Bad news travels fast, and word soon got around that she had deserted her church and home. Her mother found a hastily written note, which said, "I am tired of the humdrum life I am living. I have joined a wandering theatrical troupe as their singer."

The weeks stretched into months—the months into years, but no word reached the broken-hearted parents of the missing girl. Surely, someday their faith would be rewarded.

Almost ten years later the same congregation had assembled for worship. The vacationing choir director had been unable to supply substitute music for this particular Sunday, so the minister suggested that there might be a visiting singer in the audience who would be willing to participate. Suddenly a woman arose and walked quietly to a position beside the great organ. Following a brief conversation with the organist, she began to sing:

> "I walked through the woodland meadows,
>   Where sweet the thrushes sing;
> And found on a bed of mosses,
>   A bird with a broken wing.
> I healed its wound, and each morning
>   It sang its old sweet strain:
> But the bird with the broken pinion,
>   Never soared as high again."

A deadly stillness had settled over the congregation. They had not recognized her. The lines of dissipation had furrowed deeply,

but her voice still had the same sweet qualities
that had so endeared her to them all. The
song continued:

"I found a young life broken
    By sin's seductive art;
And touched with a Christ-like pity
    I took her to my heart.
She lived with a noble purpose,
    And struggled not in vain;
But the life that sin had stricken,
    Never soared as high again.

"But the bird with a broken pinion
    Kept another from the snare;
And the life that sin had stricken
    Raised another from despair.
Each loss has its compensation,
    There is healing for every pain;
But the bird with a broken pinion
    Never soars as high again.

"But the soul that comes to Jesus
    Is saved from every sin,
And the heart that fully trusts Him
    Shall a crown of glory win;
Then come to the dear Redeemer,
    He'll cleanse you from every stain.

By His wonderful love and mercy,
　　You shall surely rise again."

The atmosphere was tense. It was Bonnie who broke the spell.

"I was the bird with the broken wing. I wandered far from the teachings of my parents and my church. I turned my back on the teachings of Jesus and deliberately sought excitement in questionable places. Eventually I fell so low as to become a singer in cheap night clubs and foul smelling bar-rooms.

"One night I wandered past a street meeting on skid row. A young girl was singing this song I just finished. She sang of the love of Jesus. For the first time I saw a ray of hope for me. The last verse is a reality to me— by His wonderful love and mercy, I have risen again."

In my reading somewhere I once found the beautiful story of a wondrous stream which possessed the rare power of making white everything that came in touch with its waters. The little pebbles in the bottom of the channel were perfectly white. The flowers that ornamented its banks and sometimes kissed its surface were white as snow. The birds that loved its cool shades and bathed in its waters came forth from their baptism with a ray of light. A bar of iron, left for a time in its bosom, became as a bar of finest silver. All of this was because of peculiar mineral qualities found in the source from which it flowed.

"God paints in many colors," says a noted writer, "but he never paints so gorgeously as when He paints in white." However, the divine art is at its best in portrayal of the cleansed and transformed life.

"Come now, and let us reason together, saith Lord: though your sins be as scarlet, they shall be as white as snow: though they be red like crimson, they shall be as wool."

| Chapter Eight | PRAISE CHANGES THINGS |

MANY HOMES DISPLAY the motto, PRAYER CHANGES THINGS, and great blessing has resulted from this simple statement. We are all aware that prayer does change things. We know, also, that many times the enemy has not been moved one inch from his stronghold, although we have persisted in prayer for days, months—yes, often years.

Such was my own experience when passing through a time of very great pressure, and prayer did not change things. I came into possession of a wonderful secret. That secret is simply this: after we have prayed and believed, PRAISE CHANGES THINGS.

One morning during the summertime a fellow-missionary, who was then a guest in our home, went out into the garden for a stroll among the flowers. He returned after a short time holding in his hand a lovely white pigeon that he had found beside the garden walk. One of its wings was injured and it could not fly. The missionary became greatly interested in its welfare, building a coop from an old wooden box to shelter it from the weather, and feeding it morning, noon and night. As the days passed, the pigeon became quite tame. It would watch its mates as they soared away up through the heaven's blue, making no attempt to use its wings and follow them in their flight. Poor little bird with a broken wing! Our hearts were knit to the wee thing in tender sympathy, for were we not also prisoners?

Prayer had gone up from our hearts almost unceasingly: one long, yearning cry for deliverance from the bondage which held us. Not one rift in the cloud could we discern. Although our "prayer-wing" was fully developed, we were like the little bird—BOUND. We do praise God, that throughout those dark days we were kept from fainting. Faith ever beheld a star of hope!

Our loving Lord drew our attention at this time to an altogether new line of attacking the enemy. His Word unfolded step by step, and such a revelation of the secret of obtaining victory was given that our prayer life underwent a complete transformation. We discovered that two wings were necessary to mount the soul God-ward: Prayer, Praise. Prayer asks. Praise takes, or obtains the answer.

I am sure that some who read these lines may say, "I, too, have prayed and prayed, but I do not feel like praising God. Praise when my heart is bleeding and torn? Praise when the pressure is greatest? Praise when walking through the valley of the shadow with the one I have loved better than my own life? How can I praise God at such a time?"

In Psalms 107:22 we find these words: "*Sacrifice . . . the sacrifice of thanksgiving.*" What is a sacrifice? It is an offering to God. A "sacrifice of thanksgiving" is to praise God when you do not feel like it; when you are depressed and despondent; when your life is covered with thick clouds and midnight darkness.

While we are admonished to "pray without ceasing," are we not also commanded to "rejoice evermore?"

When shall I praise God? When I feel happy and when everything is moving along smoothly? When there is no trial crossing my pathway? It would be no sacrifice to praise God at such a time as this. Sacrifice hurts! It costs!

The book of Jonah contains a very precious truth which throws a great deal of light upon this subject. No one could have been in a place where the outlook was darker. Jonah was at the bottom of the sea with the *"weeds wrapped about his head."* What a desperate situation! Humanly speaking, every ray of hope was gone, and he said, *"My soul fainted within me."* But listen! In his trouble he also said, *"I will look again toward thy holy temple."* He did a very sensible thing when he took his eyes off the discouraging surroundings and began to pray. He then went a step further and determined to praise without feeling, saying, *"I will sacrifice with the voice of thanksgiving."* What a place for a praise meeting! And what a song! *"Salvation (deliverance) is of the Lord!"* As he sang and praised, the great whale began to rise toward the surface of the water, move out toward the shore, and Jonah soon found himself upon the dry land.

Praise has a wonderful lifting power! We need not be anxious about the outcome of things if we will but take the attitude of deliverance and begin to praise. When Jonah's soul fainted within him, he deliberately looked away from his impossible surroundings and uttered these wonderful words: *"They that observe lying vanities forsake their own mercy."* Let us note this lesson: when Jonah was hemmed in on every side, everything that he could see which suggested disaster he called a "lying vanity." If he had not taken his eyes off these "lying vanities," he would have forsaken the mercy that God offered him. We never get faith by looking at ourselves, our surroundings and our difficulties.

We read in 1 Samuel of Saul being tormented by an evil spirit. David was sent for, and the record says, *"When David played upon his harp the evil spirit left Saul and he was well."* Is not this a splendid way of getting rid of the enemy when he attacks us with mental depression?

Martin Luther once wrote these words, "When I cannot pray, I always sing."

It is said that there is not one despondent note to be found in the New Testament.

In 2 Chronicles there is a thrilling narrative concerning a battle won through praise. Jehoshaphat was told that a great multitude was coming against him from across the sea. He fully realized the difficulty of the situation and went to the Lord with his trouble. His was a humble prayer: *"We have no might against this great company . . . neither know we what to do: but our eyes are upon Thee."* Not upon the greatness of the difficulty, but upon Him. It was a crucial test, but the Lord did not leave Jehoshaphat in doubt as to His will. He made it known through one of the young men, who spoke these words of the Lord: *"The battle is not yours but God's . . . ye shall not need to fight . . . fear not, nor be dismayed."*

Fear is a deadly enemy. Let us remember, when we are tempted to tremble that *"God hath not given us the spirit of fear; but of power, and of love, and of a sound mind."* (2 Timothy 1:7)

Then, Jehoshaphat appointed singers who should go forth before the army singing, *"Praise the Lord, for his mercy endureth forever."* They did this even though there was not one visible sign of the promised salvation of the Lord. Right in the very face of battle— against an army mighty in number, they sang *"Praise the Lord!"* The inspired record says: *"When they began to sing and to praise, the Lord set ambushments against the children of Ammon, Moab, and Mount Seir . . . and they were smitten."* Two of the allied opposing armies began to fight the third, and when they had demolished them, they turned upon each other until the valley was filled with dead bodies and "none escaped." They had more than victory, for we read, *"Jehoshaphat and his people . . . were three days in gathering of the spoil, it was so much."* They were much richer at the end of the trial than at the beginning. They had added good which they had never dreamed of possessing.

There are two songs in Jehoshaphat's great battle: the song of praise before; the song of deliverance afterwards. We, also, should have two songs: a song in the valley of Berachab (blessing), praising God for the fulfillment of all that He has promised; but it is more precious to have the song of praise before—praising Him without sight or feeling while we see Him set ambushments against the enemy and complete the victory. Shall we not have both?

The marvelous experience which Paul and Silas had while in prison is but another example of the result of *praise at midnight*. They were bound in an inner prison. Their feet were secured in stocks because they had preached salvation through Jesus Christ. Such preaching always stirs up opposition and brings persecution, for the enemy does not wish any invasion of his territory. There was no earthly way of escape for them, and it looked as if they would lose their lives the next day. But there is always a Divine way out of a difficulty! No matter how great the difficulty may seem, we have the sure promise made by the unfailing Promiser, *"But God ... will, with the temptation (testing) also make a way of escape ..."* (1 Corinthians 10:13). The God of the impossible can make ways where there are no ways. Do we hear Paul and Silas complaining of the hardness of the way? Are they grumbling, weeping, wondering why the Lord has allowed them to get into this peculiar predicament? Definitely not. No sound of murmuring came through those prison walls. In their uncomfortable position, their backs bleeding from the wounds inflicted by the thongs, they praised God and offered unto Him the "sacrifice of thanksgiving." Perhaps their duet ran something like this:

> "His grace is sufficient for me,
>   His grace is sufficient for me,
>   His strength is made perfect in weakness,
>   His grace is sufficient for me."

As they sang and praised, the miracle was wrought! The foundation of that dingy old prison began to tremble, the building rocked and swayed, the doors burst open and they were free! *"Every one's bands were loosed!"* Thus the Lord takes the things that are against us and transforms them into blessings for ourselves and others, even using our enemies to fight for us.

Beloved, is it a midnight time in your life? Are you in a dungeon? Are your feet held fast in the stocks? Have you given up in hopeless despair, thinking that escape is impossible? Begin, right now, to praise God! *"Whoso offereth the sacrifice of thanksgiving, glorifieth Me, and prepareth a way that I may show him the salvation of God."* (Psalms 50:23—Margin R.V.) God's word is true! When you begin to praise, He will send the earthquake and set you free!

We read in the book of Joshua how the walls of Jericho fell flat after they were compassed about seven days. God had declared that He had given them the city. Faith reckoned this to be true, so they began their march around the walls using as their only weapon that which indicated triumph—a ram's horn! Unbelief might have prayed this kind of prayer, "O Lord, make the walls totter just a little, or loosen a few stones so that we may have a sign that Thou art going to answer our prayer, and then we will praise Thee." Prudence might have said, "It is not safe to shout until the victory is actually won, lest the Lord be dishonored before the people and we be greatly humiliated." This would not have been faith at all. They acted on the authority of God's Word and shouted the shout of faith before there was a sign of encouragement, and the Lord accomplished the rest. It is after we make a full commitment that "He will bring it to pass."

How many walls of difficulty would fall flat were we to simply march around them with shouts of praise? As we compass walls with praise, the Lord has promised to "compass us about with songs of deliverance."

There is a legend which tells of two angels who come from Heaven every morning and go on their rounds all the day long. One is the Angel of Requests. The other is the Angel of Thanksgiving. Each carries a basket. The one belonging to the Angel of Requests is soon filled to overflowing, for every one pours into it great handfuls of requests; but when the day is ended, the Angel of Thanksgiving has in his basket only two or three small contributions of gratitude.

A missionary in dark China was living a defeated life. Everything about him seemed to be touched with sadness. Although he prayed many months for victory over depression and discouragement, no answer came. His life remained quite the same. He determined to leave his post and go to an interior station where he could be quiet and spend long hours in prayer till victory was assured. Upon reaching the place, he was entertained in the home of a fellow-missionary. On the wall of his bedroom hung this motto: TRY THANKSGIVING.

The two words gripped his heart, and he thought within himself, "Have I been praying all these months and have not been praising?" He stopped and began to praise God and was greatly uplifted. Instead of hiding away to agonize in prayer, he returned immediately to his waiting native converts to tell them that "praise changes things."

I wish to add my own humble testimony to that of my fellow-missionary. It was a dark, dark night in my life when the words, *"Praise waiteth for Thee, O God, in Zion,"* were impressed upon my mind. I had been waiting in prayer for months. The months were now stretching on into years—piled up, as it were, before God. Could not I now wait in praise before I saw the answer, or must I wait for signs and wonders ere I believe His Word? God was waiting for me to take this final step in faith, and when I began to praise Him for the answer, to wait in praise, to "rest in the Lord, and wait patiently for Him," He began to answer in a manner that was "exceeding abundantly above all" that I could ask or think. The possession of the secret of victory has transformed my life and filled it with unutterable gladness.

This story is told of Sir Michael Costa. He was holding a rehearsal one night with his vast array of musicians and hundreds of voices. The mighty chorus rang out with thunder of organ, sounding of horns and clashing of cymbals. Far back in the orchestra one who played the piccolo said to himself, "In all this din it matters not what I do." Suddenly, all was still! The great conductor had stopped. Someone had failed to take his part! The sweet note of the piccolo had been missed.

"Let all the people praise thee, O God; let all the people praise Thee. Then shall the earth yield her increase and God, even our own God shall bless us." (Psalms 67: 5, 6)

Is your "praise note" missing from the heavenly choir? Are you waiting, waiting, yearning for God to answer your prayer? He is waiting to answer.

Try thanksgiving.

Rejoice in the Lord always, and again I say rejoice.

Chapter Nine	REDISCOVER-ING GOD

"The greatest undeveloped resource of our country is Faith; the greatest unused power is Prayer." Roger Babson.

More than anything else that may be needed at this hour, more than changed conditions, more than release from pressure, is a vigorous faith in God—a rediscovery of Him who knows the paths of a hundred million stars and knows the way through every valley of difficulty and over every mountain of trial.

What are we to do in the face of circumstances that test and try the stoutest heart?

Renew our confidence in God; rediscover God, the mighty God—a match for mighty needs. We have been brought, many of us, into circumstances in which our past conception of God is inadequate. We need a renewal of confidence.

David, the Psalmist, passed through a period fraught with devastating darkness, trial and testing. Again and again he was tempted to give up in despair—to lie down and die. Some of the Psalms fairly quaver with a cry of agony accompanied by a prayer for a way of escape. But in the twenty-seventh Psalm we find the secret which sustained him. "*I had fainted, unless I had believed to see the goodness of the Lord in the land of the living.*"

Abraham believed God when everything witnessed to the contrary. The moving biography of this great man of faith throbs with the poignancy of the humanly impossible extremities and situations in which he so often found himself. It was in those dark places that he was taught the strength of omnipotence.

Moses "endured as seeing Him who is invisible!" Think of his forty years of endurance; his desert experience! One, five, or even ten years would have seemed long enough, but, without any explanation, God prolonged the testing; and then, one day Moses heard a Voice! It came as a surprise—a discovery. His desert isolation training period was ended and shortly we see him standing on the shores of the Red Sea as he leads the restless hordes of Israel in their flight from Egypt. They are in a terrifying position—bounded on the north by the desert, on the south by the desert, on the west by Pharaoh's army, and on the east by the Red Sea. Surely this was enough to chill any heart with despair, but Moses looked up and saw that God was there, boundless in His all-power, all-wisdom and all-grace.

Habakkuk shouted God's praises when he saw the vines without fruit, the fields burned and bare, the stalls without herds. He rejoiced because he had faith in God. It was his audacious certitude of faith that made him the prophet of all ages.

An exciting story of supernatural deliverance is recorded in 2 Kings 4. A minister's widow was suddenly placed in an inextricable web of circumstances. In accordance with the custom of the time, the creditors came to take away her two sons. These sons were doubtless wage-earners and provided a living for their mother. What now was she to do? She took her two sons and went to her Lord and shut the door. There in her very humble cottage she cried to One who ever hears the heart-cry of the widow. God was listening.

How it would stimulate our faith if we could visit that widow's cottage and learn from her what God did on her behalf when every visible prop was gone. I believe that she would testify to the fact that she found the hardest place in life was the *sweetest* place, for it was there she made a fresh discovery of God.

In our day it seems that evil forces are sweeping every vestige of good away. It oft-times appears that God's clean sun of right-eousness has set permanently into the unsee-able, distant horizon. It is at just such times as this that the staying hand of our patient Heav-enly Father moves back and forth across the limitless universe, touching here and there those in whom He has confidence, using them as eternal heralds to point the way back to God, and defining in practical terms the way of rediscovery and renewal.

A most unusual incident occurred in color-ful Mexico City a few years ago. A famous artist had painted a beautiful picture, and it was being displayed upon the walls of a new, ultra-modern hotel. The scene was of one of the charming beauty spots of the country land-scape. It depicted with lucid clarity the roll-ing country landscape, quiet fields, purling streams and a touch of virgin forest, carpeted with gorgeous flowers.

Across the top of the canvas four words were painted which stood out in bold outline. They were these: "God Does Not Exist." A strange bit of lettering to be found on such a famous work of art!

Spellbound visitors surged past the painting every day.

One evening a large group of young men entered the lobby of the hotel and made their way down the corridor to the room that housed the painting. They quietly and calmly removed paint cans and brushes from kits strapped to their shoulders and were soon busily at work. No one but those in the room could see what was going on; the air was freighted with suspense. Suddenly they stepped back and again the throng pressing against the doorway caught a glimpse of the masterpiece. At first they could see no change, but continued scrutiny revealed that three words in the caption had been brushed completely from the canvas, and what were the words? "Does Not Exist." One word remained—"God."

The group quietly, but with the stride of conquerors, left the hotel. The onlookers stared in awe. Under the soft lights which were thrown upon the picture, that one glorious word was emblazoned—it shone like a brilliant in a monarch's crown.

A second look revealed a new light beginning to glow in the eyes of the thoughtful watchers. Surely here were the first fruits of rediscovery.

A memorable dinner was reported in London more than fifty years ago. It was given by Christopher Neville for some of the leaders of English thought—leaders in politics, literature, finance, art and religion. Following the dinner, Dean Stanley proposed a discussion of the question, "Who will dominate the future?" He called upon Professor Huxley to speak first. The professor arose and indicated that in his opinion the future would be dominated by the nation that adhered most closely to the facts. The audience was profoundly impressed.

After a moment of silence, the Dean again arose and called upon an English journalist, who was also a member of Parliament and President of the Royal Commission of Education. Beginning quietly, he went on to say, "Gentlemen, I have been listening to the last speaker with profound interest and I agree with him in his premise that the future will belong to the nation which sticks to the facts. But I want to add one word—*all the facts*, not just some of them. The greatest fact of history," he continued, "is God."

Spiritual paralysis disappears in the presence of spiritual rediscovery. The forces of the night are so imminent—the magnitude of the crisis is so great that many are being tempted to cry out with the disciples, "*Lord, carest thou not that we perish?*" Yet He who may appear to be "asleep upon a pillow" is riding upon the storm in all His Divine majesty. We gain reassurance through the Psalmist, "*Cast thy burden upon the Lord, and He shall sustain thee: he shall never suffer the righteous to be moved."*

Our great need is for a vital faith in the omnipotent God. When oppressed with staggering problems, do not consider their boundaries, but rediscover the boundlessness of God.

<table>
<tr><td>Chapter
Ten</td><td># DARE TO BE
DEFINITE WITH
GOD</td></tr>
</table>

ONE COLD WINTER, many years ago, the people of a certain town were in great trouble. A hostile army was marching down upon them, and they were certain that the brutal soldiers would ravage their homes. In one family there was an aged grandmother. While the other members of her family were paralyzed by fear and worry, she was praying that God would protect them by building a wall of defense round about them.

During the night they heard the tramping of many feet and the clanking of heavy artillery, but no harm came to them. In the morning they moved cautiously out of the house. To the utter amazement of everyone except the grandmother, they discovered that a huge wall of drifted snow stood between their house and the road. The plundering army had missed a rich prize by only a few feet.

"See," said the grandmother, "God did build a wall around us!"

This stirring story underlines with emphatic clarity the secret of a happy Father-child relationship with our God through prayer. A contemporary scientist has said that the greatest untapped power in the world today is spiritual—the power of prayer. It must be remembered, however, that prayer is impotent unless it is both definite and urgent. So many prayers are offered in a spirit which really says, "I will not be grieved if the answer does not come soon; and, in fact, if it does not come at all, I will not be greatly disappointed." Such prayers represent little more than a pious wish and only tend to limit God in what He would like to do for us. This is aptly expressed in the following four lines by Hazel H. Simon:

You limit Him so! You limit Him so!
Trust God, and a childlike faith will grow,
For grace and goodness are in His hand,
And the powers of Heaven at your command!

Our Bible is fluent in answers to definite and prevailing prayer. Abraham's servant prays—Rebekah appears. Jacob wrestles and prays—Esau's mind is wonderfully turned from the revengeful purpose he has harbored for twenty years. Moses prays—the Red Sea divides. Joshua prays—Achan is discovered. Isaiah prays—the dream is revealed. Daniel prays—the lions are muzzled. Nehemiah starts a prayer—the king's heart is softened in a minute. Elijah prays—a drought of three years succeeds. Elijah prays again—rain descends in torrents. Elisha prays—the Jordan is divided. The New Testament church prays ardently—Peter is delivered from prison by an angel.

Again and again, the writers of the Bible seem to delight in fixing our gaze upon the difficulties which lie in the way of the people of God—magnifying, almost unnecessarily, the obstacles to deliverance, and then, in the most striking and arresting manner, showing God in command, issuing orders and leading them to triumph.

No indeed, there can be no question as to the power of prayer to control situations in which mighty deeds are done, any more than there can be the slightest doubt of its importance in Christian life and work. Scripture abounds with graphic illustrations of prayer battles fought amid the strangest surroundings, proving the might of weakness when allied to God.

Most of us readily assent to the truth of the Biblical record regarding the importance of definite and urgent prayer, but we are seemingly inclined to feel that God just does not do things that way any more. Many thrill-packed stories come to us from the last war. This one received little publicity at the time, but it is a potent illustration of one who "dared to be definite."

The crew of a flying fortress had to take to their life rafts after being forced down at sea while en route to Australia on a routine mission. Eight of the nine crewmen were greatly worried. The ninth, Sergeant Hernandez, began to pray. Shortly thereafter, he startled the rest of the crew by announcing that help was on the way. He continued to pray. At the end of the second day they were rescued by native

Australian fishermen near a lonely coral island. These natives had been several hundred miles from the mainland in their outrigger canoes and had turned homeward with their catch, when a "strange urge came over them." Something impelled them to alter their course and steer for the worthless, uninhabited little coral island where the airmen had drifted.

Yes, prayer has as much power today as it ever had. God has not changed. *"Behold, the Lord's hand is not shortened, that it cannot save; neither his ear heavy, that it cannot hear."* Prayer is the key that unlocks all of the storehouses of God's infinite grace and power—it can do anything that God can do, and since God can do anything, prayer is omnipotent.

Let us now be very practical. Prayer is an exceedingly necessary exercise in our spiritual growth. It brings us into fellowship with God. Sir Isaac Newton once said, "I can take my telescope and look millions of miles into space; but I can go away to my room, and in prayer, get nearer to God and heaven than I can when assisted by all of the telescopes in the world." Such companionship completely drives out petty wants and trivial desires and brings us to the place of unreserved surrender to the Divine will. The life surrendered in prayer may well be likened to the beautiful bamboo trees. Bamboo is one of the most useful plants in the Orient. It is hollow; it has what the Chinese people call an "empty heart." When it is cut, it becomes a channel through which something else may flow. God's grace and power flow freely through the "bamboo-like" life.

Again, prayer is a powerful instrument for use in our relationship with others, but all too often, we suffer defeat by not "daring to be definite." Remember, God has no use for pessimists in prayer. "*Ye have not because ye ask not*," is the Spirit's explanation for failure to get results. "Expect great things from God, and you will get them," is the sober and triumphant verdict of George Mueller, the latter-day apostle of prevailing prayer. Surely, since we have all of the resources of the Saviour on which to draw, we may safely be the most habitual optimists in prayer. To the ardent soul who would excel in prayer, pessimism is a state of mind that needs to be consciously and constantly guarded against.

Daring and definite prayer is the appointed means by which rivers of energy are unsealed and directed to desperate needs; therefore, vital prayer is not a word—it is an act! It is as much an act as a waterman's lifting of a sluicegate that lets the higher waters into the lock where the rivers are low. Prayer prepares the way for the supply of the Spirit of Christ, and in that holy energy we have the power which over-matches and conquers difficulties that are otherwise invincible.

Prayer prevails. It brings power. It brings life. It brings God. Let us dare to be definite with God; let us dare to lay hold of the promises and to wait in faith until the answer comes.

> Those who are quite sure God lives,
> Cannot have a lonely day!
> Those who are quite sure God loves,
> Show His love upon life's way!
> Those who are quite sure God sees,
> See Him also everywhere!
> Those who are quite sure God hears,
> Often speak to Him in prayer!

| *Chapter* | **UNFAILING** |
| *Eleven* | **SPRINGS** |

A MOST UNUSUAL story is found in the first chapter of Judges. Achsah had received a gift of land from her father. As she surveyed her new holdings, she discovered, much to her consternation, that there were no water wells —the land was a barren waste.

Achsah sent word to her father that she would like to see him. She was called into his presence and was greeted with the question, "*What wilt thou, my daughter?*" Her reply was definite. "*Thou hast given me a south land; give me also springs of water.*" Her request was granted immediately. Caleb gave her the "*upper and the nether springs.*"

This generous gift exceeded her fondest expectations; the land would now become fruitful and fertile. It was then evident that she had learned early one of life's greatest lessons—

if a blessing is to be enjoyed, it must be shared. Others should have the opportunity of quenching their thirst from these flowing springs. She sent out this invitation to her neighbors, "*Come ye to the waters, come, and drink abundantly. . . .*"

The Psalmist gave his testimony and left these wonderful words on record, "*They thirsted not when he led them through the deserts. He turned the dry land into springs of water. He gave them drink as out of the great depths.*" As they walked through the wilderness and desert wastes, He filled their cups—not from a little cistern, but as from some illimitable ocean. You cannot exhaust the springs fed from the deeps. "*They drank of that spiritual rock that followed them: and that Rock was Christ.*" He holds an exhaustless supply for all the millions of the earth.

Achsah might have been content with a dry, barren land, but how much better that she had the faith to say, "Give me a blessing."

Without these springs of water, how barren the life! On the day of the great feast, Jesus said, "*If any man thirst let him come unto me and drink. He that believeth on me, as the Scripture hath said, out of his inner being shall flow rivers of living water. (But this spake he of the Spirit, which they that believe on him should receive: for the Holy Ghost was not yet given because that Jesus was not yet glorified.)"* John 7:37, 38, 39. Again, He said, *"Whosoever drinketh of the water that I shall give him shall be in him a well of water springing up into everlasting life."* John 4:14.

No simpler, stronger symbol of the Spirit could be found than this, a Spring—a Well-Spring—never dry—never turbid; from its clear depths, fed through the secret veins of earth, it gushes ever into life. It goes not downward, but it springs up and it flows out.

"All my fresh springs are in Thee," said David. The soul that has found all its springs in God never knows its supply to fail or vary; we need both *upper and nether springs*. The Spirit of God in the highest regions of life and down to its lowest level—the need is still the same.

An eastern caravan was overtaken once in the desert with a failure of the water supply.

The accustomed fountains were all dried; the oasis was a desert. They stopped an hour before sunset to find, after a day of scorching heat, that they were perishing for want of water. Vainly they explored the usual wells, but they were all dry. Dismay was upon all faces; despair was in all hearts. Suddenly an old man approached the sheik and advised him to unloose the two beautiful deer that he was taking home as a present to his bride. Surely the sensitive nostrils of the deer would detect the presence of water if any was to be found. Their tongues were protruding with thirst; their bosoms heaved with distress, but as they were led out to the borders of the camp, they lifted up their heads and sniffed the air. Then, with unerring instinct, with a course as straight as an arrow and speed as swift as the wind, they darted off across the desert. Swift horsemen followed close behind, and an hour or two later hastened back with the good news that water had been found. The camp moved with shouts of rejoicing to the newly discovered fountains.

To the heart that is hungering and thirsting after God and His fullness—for a drink from the living springs, this promise will be found literally true: *"When the poor and needy seek water and there is none, and their tongue faileth for thirst, I the Lord will hear them ... I will open rivers in high places and fountains in the midst of the valleys. I will make the dry land springs of water."* Isaiah 41:17-21.

Come, thirsty one, bring your cup of need to God's measureless supply. Come and drink. Yes, drink abundantly.

> Though millions their thirst now are slaking,
>   It never runs dry:
> And millions may still come partaking,
>   It never runs dry.

Chapter Twelve | HARVEST SECRETS

TRAGEDY HAD STRUCK at the very heart of the British Empire—one of her favorite sons lay still in death. The Duke of Wellington, once invincible in battle, now lay lifeless in the great hall, surrounded only by those vigilant sentries who maintained their final watch.

Dignitaries journeyed from every dominion and protectorate to pay tribute to their fallen hero and statesman, and a special section was established in the great cathedral for the chosen representative of every military unit of the vast colonial army—every regiment of every country flying the Union Jack would stand in final homage to their great leader.

One of the greatest imperatives of the Gospel rings with undisguised urgency as it expresses the supreme wish of the Saviour to be represented in His great Kingdom by members of every tribe and nation. The Master gave vivid expression of this burning desire as He stood on the verdant mountain, high above glimmering Galilee and spoke the words that have dominated Christian thought for centuries, *"Go ye therefore, and teach all nations...."*

How anxious Jesus is that all men have the opportunity to hear the glad message, *"Come unto me ... and I will give you rest,"* but, in the words of Matthew, *"The harvest truly is plenteous, but the laborers are few."*

A Christian young man stood one day for several hours before a breathtakingly beautiful picture in a Chicago art gallery. He seemed completely oblivious to the passing of time as he studied every detail of the great work of art.

The picture, that was demanding so much of him, portrayed in bold hues a striking autumn scene. Standing in the midst of a large furrowed field were row on row of stately shocks of gathered grain. The golden glow of sunset and a hush of peace, that comes only after the toil of the day, fell like a mantle over the entire scene.

The gallery guard had noticed the absorption of the young man for some time. Finally, he stepped up, tapped him on the shoulder and asked, "What does that picture say to you?"

"God must have wanted to produce a harvest and needed grains of wheat for that purpose. He asked them to make a complete surrender of themselves. In so doing, those golden shocks became a reality."

Herein lies the great secret of the fulfilment of the Master's last command: "*He that loseth his life for my sake, shall find it.*" Again, "*Except a corn of wheat fall into the ground and die it abideth alone, but if it die, it bringeth forth much fruit.*"

A cry from the heart of black slaves reached the throne of God. Dark Africa stretched forth her dusky hands beseeching Him for help. God heard, but to answer their cry for help He needed a human voice. An angel could not carry to the black man the sweet story of the matchless love of God. A young Scotchman sat at his loom weaving—he heard a faint cry—a cry as of pain. He heard it in the stillness of the night; he heard it through the cacophonies of day-time city life. Should he leave home and friends to bury himself amid Africa's wilds? The whole wide world knows the answer, for David Livingstone gave of himself on Africa's soil. The harvest of his life may be seen in the countless multitude of Africa's sons and daughters who have been "transformed into His likeness."

The Lord of the harvest wanted to sow a great field with living seeds in age-old China. He needed a sower. One Sunday morning He found Hudson Taylor walking by the seashore. He spoke to him saying, "If you will let Me, I will walk all over China through you." On that day of days a grain of wheat fell into the ground and died. Multiplied thousands of living grains are the result.

The following is a reprint of a letter received by an African missionary: "I, Kalamba, the king of Lulua, have long been a seeker after life. I have gone west as far as the Great Waters, but the Portuguese satisfied me not. I went to the east and the Belgians gave me guns which said, 'I take life, but do not give it.' I have sought to the south, but the wizards comforted me not. Passers-by have declared your Gospel to me, and I am satisfied at last. My searchings are ended. I and my people are yours. Accept as a guarantee my own child whom I am sending you, but come quickly here to my own home where we await you. Your God make you merciful to me!"

Calls and letters like this are almost commonplace in these days of unparalleled opportunity. It would appear that the task is almost impossible—even with the utilization of modern facilities, but the greatest of all of the harvest secrets is to be found in the closing words of Jesus' great command, ". . . *lo, I am with you always. . . .*"

God never asks the impossible—He is never unreasonable. He assures us that He is always with us, no matter how difficult or hard the job. The victory secured on Golgotha's peak guarantees sustained victory for us every moment of every day. We are not left to our own devices. When He gives us the command "to go," we know He will go along too.

There is a fascinating legend concerning a tribe of North American Indians who roamed in the neighborhood of Niagara. Each year they offered a young virgin as a sacrifice to the Spirit of the Mighty River. She was called "The Bride of the Falls."

The lot fell one year to a beautiful girl who was the only daughter of an old chieftain. The news was carried to him while he was sitting in his tent; but on hearing it, the old man just went on smoking his old pipe in complete silence.

On the day set aside for the sacrifice, a white canoe, full of ripe fruit and decked with flowers was ready and waiting for "The Bride." At the appointed hour she took her place in the frail bark. It was pushed out into mid-stream, where it would be carried swiftly towards the mighty cataract.

Suddenly, to the amazement of the breathless crowd, a second canoe was seen to dart out from the river bank—in it was seated the old chieftain. He paddled with swift and powerful strokes towards the swirling sacrificial canoe. He reached it, gripped it firmly, and held it fast.

The eyes of father and daughter met in one

last look of love; and then, close together, they were carried by the racing current until they plunged over the thundering cataract and perished side by side.

The father was "IN IT" with his child!

The fields are white; the harvest is ready. The Spirit of the living God is with us.

It must be remembered, however, that not all are commissioned literally to go forth to the fields afar. A great company must stand in the homeland as the rear-guards, but everyone must become buried grains—their consecration and surrender is just as real and as deep as that of those called to the far places of the world.

In this great era of world development, let us yield up our grains of wheat unto the death, and then our glorious Lord will cause us to know the power of His resurrection! Life abundant will be ours, and an undreamed of fruitage.

> Oh! struggle not to "abide,"
>   Nor labor to "bring forth fruit,"
> But let Jesus unite thee to Himself
>   As the vine-branch to the root.

So simple, so deep, so strong,
  That union with Him shall be,
His life shall forever replace thine own,
  And His love shall flow through thee.

Freda Hanbury Allen

| Chapter Thirteen | # TRUST IN THE DARK—TRIUMPH AT DAWN |

THE FOLLOWERS of Jesus of Nazareth were plunged into the depths of despair and confusion. For over three years they had followed Him faithfully and without question. His miraculous feats and amazing pronouncements had often given them the assurance that He was not just a man—he was indeed the Son of God! Of late, however, an ominous cloud of distrust and suspicion had hovered over them. An evil premonition had filled their waking moments with dread—their very foundations were jarred loose from their formerly secure moorings. Then, to their utter amazement, Jesus was arrested, brought to trial and condemned to death. Now the sentence had been executed.

The disciples had been so certain that He

would either receive a last minute reprieve or that He would strike dead those who scourged and shamed Him with such undisguised venomous hate, but miraculous deliverance did not come. They saw the mob lay upon His shoulders the heavy cross and beheld Him fainting beneath the load. They heard him cry, *"My God, my God, why hast thou forsaken me?"* They saw Him die! When all was over and His broken body was taken to the rock-hewn tomb and the door securely fastened, they stood by as creatures benumbed. Their Master, who in past months had unstopped deaf ears, opened blind eyes, and had even brought life to dead bodies, had been conquered by their evil and sinister opposition.

This was the darkest hour of their lives, for it was the end of all their hopes—even their faith had failed! Someone has well said, "When you lose your sky, you lose your earth." This is a dangerous attitude. When despair fills the heart, it provides fertile soil for the seeds of unbelief and doubt—they had trusted Him so implicitly, proving the reality of their trust by leaving all to become His followers; but now

He had forsaken them! What answer could they give to the adversary who now taunted them? Did God not care that their hearts were broken? Did He not feel their hearts throbbing with anguish through those long nights of agony?

Yes, He cared—and He loved, for, *"Having loved His own, He loved them to the end."* It did matter to Him about them, for their names were engraved upon His hands, and He carried them upon His great loving heart. However, He permitted their darkness to deepen into Egyptian blackness, for He was preparing them for heartbreaks of joy which were soon to follow. Their night of tragedy would soon end in a morning of unrivaled beauty and happiness.

Christians of all ages have passed through similar experiences. God permits these testings when He is planning fresh revelations of Himself. Wonderful surprises await those who go with Him through the Garden of Gethsemane and up steep Calvary. St. John was led to Patmos, the island of buried hopes, that God might give him a glorious revelation of unutterable magnificence and immeasurable importance.

"Where was God when this tragedy of Calvary was being enacted?" asked a perplexed person. "Was not the face of God turned away from His own beloved Son?"

He was standing behind in the shadows keeping watch above His own. Absence of joy does not mean absence of God. His eye was on the minute hand of the clock until His purpose was accomplished and the great plan of salvation wrought. God never allows His children to remain in the darkness of perplexity except "*for a season if need be.*"

Modern life presents seeming insurmountable problems and obstacles to effective and purposeful living. Fear and distrust hover over us with portentous intent. The pressures of existence force us to our knees in frustration and confusion. The powers of darkness seem to overwhelm, and like the disciples of old, we cry, "Is there no way out?"

Yes, there is a way—God's way! We find infallible direction in Isaiah 50:10: "*Who is among you that feareth the Lord, that obeyeth*

*the voice of his servant, that walketh in dark-
ness, and hath no light? Let him trust in the
name of the Lord, and stay upon his God."*
Stand still and trust. Refuse every suggestion
of the enemy to doubt, and crucify the word
"why."

The only thing about which we need to be
concerned is to be on the King's highroad, and
when a crossroad is reached, to wait patiently,
for God has set His signposts on all of life's
strange and winding roads. He is able to reveal
Himself to us according to our special need at
any particular time. He knows when we need
a special visitation to cover all of the future
with beauty and power. Often He keeps His
way hidden until just before He opens it, and
then immediately it is all unrolled like a scroll.
It does no good to struggle for a premature un-
folding of the Divine mystery; the revelation
awaits our arrival at a certain place on the road.
When time brings us to that place and we enter into its experience, we shall find to our
happy surprise that it has become luminous.

Think back to that first resurrection morning. We read, *"They came . . . at the rising of*

the sun," between dawn and daybreak, while it was still dark. They came with heavy hearts that were burdened with grief, but at daybreak they found the empty tomb and heard the glad message that night was over and their Lord had overcome death and conquered the grave. Hurriedly they returned along the very same road over which they came—utterly changed men and women.

How rewarding it is to wait patiently for God's "afters." *After* the midnight, morning will greet us. *After* sadness, joy will appear. *After* the storm, sunlight will meet us. *After* a period of severe testing, God will meet us in a very special way.

God's moments are worth waiting for—implicit trust through life's dark moments brings inexpressible triumph in the dawn.

Chapter	# GOD NEEDS
Fourteen	# YOU!

THE NAME, Stradivari, is synonymous with rare and treasured violins. His instruments, which are now over two hundred years old, are almost worth their weight in gold—they are the treasured possessions of the masters.

In George Eliot's poem, *Stradivarius*, the old violin maker says:

"If my hand slacked,
   I should rob God—since He is fullest good,
   Leaving a blank instead of violins.
   He could not make Antonio Stradivari's violins
      Without Antonio."

I believe one of the most awesome facts of life is that *God needs me—He needs you!* Stop and think about this a moment. We readily recognize and affirm our need of God, but, all too often, we fail to realize that God needs us.

"Others may do a greater work,
    But you have your part to do;
And no one in all God's heritage
    Can do it so well as you."

God has many conditional or contingent purposes for your life but you are the deciding factor. These are purposes in which God proposes to do certain things and accomplish certain results through your cooperation—you are the deciding factor. If you cooperate, the thing will be done; if not, it will not be done. There are some things God will do apart from us, but there are also many things that He cannot accomplish without the cooperation of you and me. We hold the key that will either unlock or bar up His purposes.

In the midst of life's complexities, it is well to remind ourselves that God places in our hands tremendous power. *"All things are possible to him that believeth."* By believing—by cooperating with God, we can modify many adverse conditions. Never was God more able to meet and master every adverse condition than today. Whether He will so act may well depend on what we think, believe, pray and do. Many times we wait for God to do what He waits for *us* to do.

Dr. John Matthews, noted radio minister of past years, left with us these forceful pronouncements: "When we weary of famines and floods, pestilence and poverty, conflict and war, then these plagues shall pass into history forever. They are here because we have submitted to dread and fear. We forgot the path to prayer and the force of faith . . . God never planned any such age or hour. . . . When Moses prayed, Israel was saved; when Samuel prayed, the Philistines fled in defeat . . . when Jonah prayed, a million souls were spared. It is up to us to turn the tide; man remains the deciding factor.

"When God predicts judgment or impending disaster, it is possible that we may avert it. Unless we act, judgment will surely fall; unless we set up counter laws that will rush out to meet overwhelming evils, disaster will be the result. . . .

"Someone asks, 'If God predicts or gives His word, will not that word come to pass in face of all men may do?' Not necessarily so . . .

nothing is more harmful than the failure to distinguish between the eternal decrees of God
and His conditional purposes, which we may
further, or if need be prevent."

Yes, God needs you to be forged as a strong
link in the great chain that binds His purposes
to the whole world. If you are willing to cooperate, He will reveal to you your part in His
great program.

Equally important, however, is the vital
truth that God needs you to fulfill His purposes in your own small world—in your own
immediate sphere of influence. God needs you
to translate through your life and actions His
exhaustless love. This is a very practical thing.
Actually, there is only one of you in all the
universe, in all the centuries, and God is count-
ing on you for certain acts of love and under-
standing and witness, which no one else in all
time can do. *"Inasmuch as ye have done it
unto one of the least of these my brethren ye
have done it unto me."*

In Edwin Markham's poem, *The Shoes of
Happiness*, Conrad the Cobbler dreams that
the Master will be coming as his Guest. So

vivid was the dream that Conrad woke early in the morning and swept and cleaned the shop until it shone. He went and bought food and planned that when the Master came he would wash His feet, and kiss His hands where the cruel nails had been, and then they would dine together. He sat waiting with a fast beating heart, and when he heard the door open, he got up eagerly to greet his Guest; but it was just a beggar. Conrad gave him a pair of shoes and sent him on his way. Presently an old woman came, bent with years, and a heavy burden of faggots on her back; he made her sit down and rest and gave her some food. Conrad waited all day, and finally, late in the afternoon a child came in, crying bitterly. She was lost. He dried her tears and took her back to her mother. But the Master never came, and Conrad sobbed in his little shop with a heavy heart:

"Then soft in the silence a Voice he heard
Lift up your heart, for I've kept my word.
Three times I came to your friendly door;
Three times my shadow was on your floor.
I was the beggar with the bruised feet;

I was the woman ye gave to eat;
I was the homeless child in the street."

Marvel of marvels! God needs me! God needs you! He needs us to be His partners. In the little story entitled *The Lady of Chimney Corner*, written by a noted English writer, we find this beautiful passage concerning God's need of our hands. "God takes a hand wherever He can find it and jist diz what He likes we' it. Sometimes He takes a bishop's and lays it on a child's head in benediction; then He takes the han' of a docther t' relieve pain, th' han' of a mother t' guide her chile, an' sometimes He takes the han' of an aul craither like me t' give a bit of comfort to a neighbor. But they're all han's touched be His Spirit, an' His Spirit is every where lukin' fur han's to use."

No person is too small for God's attention— He needs you. He stoops from His Almightiness to ask our aid. Man is God's method of reaching *our* world and the *whole* world with the glorious truth that the risen Christ is eager to assume possession of men's hearts and lives. He needs us to be living sermons in a lost world that sees and knows Him not.

GOD NEEDS YOU!

And Gideon was nothing,
Was nothing in the fray,
But just a suit of working clothes
The Spirit wore that day.

	# GREAT
Chapter	# PRESSURE
Fifteen	# MEANS GREAT
	# POWER

WHAT SHOULD be the attitude of a Christian when placed in a difficult and trying situation—a place of severe testing? There can be but one attitude! A simple and unwavering trust in God! A refusal to look *at* the difficult circumstance, but *above* it. The only sure way to do this is to live very close to God. As the turbo-supercharger enables an airplane to maintain full power at an altitude of thirty thousand feet, where an ordinary plane has lost four-fifths of its power, so the Christian who walks with his God, listening and obeying, keeps strong at the toughest heights of life. The fact is that God is stronger than any temptation and danger; and the person who has God in his heart is unconquerable.

It is true, however, that God often seems to place His children in positions of profound difficulty, leading them into a tight corner— from which there is no way of escape—contriving a situation which no human judgment would have permitted.

During such periods, the words of Jesus in Mark 9:23 take on added significance. ". . . *If thou canst believe, all things are possible to him that believeth*." It should be clearly understood that this kind of faith in God is the most practical approach to the problems and testings of life—it is not sense, or sight, or reason, but taking God at His word. Experience reveals that such a faith will not make the sun rise sooner, but it will make the night seem shorter.

No derelict of skidrow presents a more tragic picture than a person in an amoral state, devoid of faith and trust. A story is told by Francis Browne of a little pilgrim band sitting by the seashore recounting their losses, while one tells of a ship that went down with all his household, and another, the sweet memories of a lost youth, and others of vanished gold, of proud honors gone, and of faithless friends; "a stranger seeming from all sorrow free," said:

> Sad losses have ye met,
> But mine is heavier yet:
> For a believing heart hath gone from me.

"Alas!" said the pilgrims: "Thine, stranger, is life's last and heaviest loss."

And the verdict is right. Life's greatest loss is the loss of faith. "Christ's anxiety to retain Peter's faith," says one writer, "can only be explained in one way. He did not interfere between him and failure, but He did interfere between him and the loss of faith. A man is lost when honor, truth and character are gone; but when faith has gone, he has suffered the greatest loss."

Such tragic waste! Our loving Heavenly Father provides the capacity to meet every need. It is true that faith deals with the supernatural, but God is anxious to transmit to each of us the ability to understand. When Dr. Patton was translating the New Testament into an island language, he found great difficulty in locating a native word for "faith."

While in his study one day, deep at work on the translation, one of his native teachers came in hot and exhausted after a long walk. He threw himself down on the cane chair, put his feet up on another, and wiping his forehead, he used a word which meant, "I'm resting my whole weight here." Instantly Dr. Patton had the word he wanted. You simply "rest your whole weight" on God day after day. Faith has nothing to rest upon but God's inviolable Word! *"Let us hold fast the profession of our faith without wavering; (for he is faithful that promised.)"* Hebrews 10:23.

A great deal of caution must be exercised at this point. A "pseudo-faith" based on "seemings" and "feelings" is often substituted for real faith. Pleasurable emotions and deep satisfying experiences are part of the Christian life, but they are not all of it. Trials, conflicts, battles and testings lie along the way, and are not to be counted as misfortunes, but rather as part of our necessary discipline. In all of these varying experiences we are to reckon on Christ as dwelling in the heart, regardless of our feelings, if we are walking obediently before Him.

Here is where many get into trouble; they try to walk by feeling rather than faith. Distinguish between the fact of God's presence, and the emotion of the fact—herein lies the eternal secret of faith.

But where is such a faith to be found? It will be born within us in some hour of desperate need, when we are driven to our very extremities. When pressed out of measure and pressed to all lengths, we will be "pressed into knowing no help but God!"

Our Master said, "*Have the faith of God.*" The faith of God is inwrought within our hearts by the Holy Spirit. In the pathway of faith we come to learn that the Lord's thoughts are not our thoughts nor His ways our ways. Both in the physical and spiritual realm, *great pressure means great power!* Although circumstance may bring us into the place of death, that need not spell disaster—for if we trust in the Lord and wait patiently, it simply provides the occasion for the display of His mighty power. Faith is not a magic drug, a spiritual anaesthetic; it is the victory that overcometh the world by doing battle with it.

Faith, mighty faith, the promise sees,
   And looks to God alone,
Laughs at impossibilities
   And cries, "It shall be done."

Chapter Sixteen

NOT OVERWORK BUT OVERFLOW

A CAMBRIDGE NATURALIST told me once of an experiment he had made with a pigeon. The bird had been born in a cage and had never been free. One day the owner took the bird out on the porch of the house and flung it into the air. To the naturalist's surprise the bird's capacity for flight was perfect. Round and round it flew as if it had been born in the air; but soon in its flight it became excited and was panting. The circles grew smaller until at last the bird dashed full against its master's breast and fell to the ground. What did it mean? It meant that, though the bird had inherited the instinct of flight it had not inherited the capacity to stop. If it had not risked the shock of a sudden halt, the little life would have panted out in the air.

Isn't that a parable of modern life?—completely endowed with the instinct of action but without the capacity to stop. Round and round life goes in its weary circle until it is almost dying at full speed. Any shock, even some severe experience, is a mercy if it checks the whirl. Sometimes God stops such a soul abruptly by some sharp blow of trouble, and the soul falls in despair at His feet. Then He bends over it and says: "Be still, my child; be still and know that I am God!"—until by degrees the despair of trouble is changed into submission and obedience, and the poor, weary, fluttering life is made strong to fly again.

Recall with me those expressive words found in Song of Solomon 1:7, *"Tell me O thou whom my soul loveth, where thou makest thy flock to rest at noon . . . ?"* The art of "resting at noon" has been lost, and many are succumbing to the strain of life which is being lived in "high gear." Rest is not a sedative for the sick, but a tonic for the strong. It spells emancipation, illumination, transformation! It saves us from becoming slaves, even of good works.

"See that your clock does not run down!" is the timely admonition sung by the colored people of the south. In my possession is an eight day clock. One night after an unusually strenuous day, when the physical was taxed to the uttermost, and we had forgotten the place where "the flocks rested at noon," we found ourselves carrying loads that belonged to the next day, the next month, the next year. Sleep wanted to take its departure—we listened to the slow and very feeble tick of this clock, and it seemed to say, "I am all run down and cannot go on much longer." It was growing fainter and fainter, and shortly would have stopped had not a voice from the adjoining room called out, "the clock is running down; someone had better get up and wind it before it stops." And, someone obeyed! After a few moments as we listened, we heard again the strong, steady tick, tick, tick. The clock had been wound and this was the result. A still, small voice spoke to my inner heart, and the haunting refrain of the Negro spiritual, "See that your clock does not run down," hummed itself into the deepest recesses of my being.

A successful business acquaintance of mine visited his doctor for a physical checkup. The doctor was appalled at the deterioration in health of his patient. His nerves were obviously tensed almost to the snapping point— he was a victim of "internal combustion." So great was his agitation that his capacity for clear and constructive thought was tragically impaired.

Following a careful diagnosis, the physician realized that the answer to my friend's need could not be scribbled on a prescription pad or removed through surgery. No, his therapy must consist of an extensive period away from the busy office. God's fresh air and golden sunshine must dust away the cobwebs that were befogging a tired mind.

He had been too busy even to attend church; too busy to pray—naturally his strength had fled. In this desperate physical and mental state he decided to attend the midweek prayer meeting to ask the people to pray for the restoration of his health. An elderly gentleman arose in this prayer meeting and gave the following testimony:

"Once I was in just the physical condition as Mr. Baker. I was all run down physically and mentally, as well as spiritually. One day I opened my Bible and read these words, *"They that wait upon the Lord shall renew their strength; they shall mount up with wings as eagles; they shall run, and not be weary; and they shall walk, and not faint."* He continued, "That was the key that unlocked the healing streams, causing fresh life to flow through my body and weary brain. I made a little sanctuary in the corner of my office into which I entered daily and waited upon the Lord, exchanging my weakness for His strength. Today at the age of seventy-five, I am stronger in every way than I was at sixty, and I am doing twice as much work, for I have learned the glorious secret: NOT OVERWORK, BUT OVERFLOW!"

Tradition tells us that one day a hunter found the Apostle John seated on the ground playing with a tame quail. The hunter expressed his surprise that a man so earnest should be spending his time so profitlessly. John looked up and asked, "Why is the bow on your shoulder unstrung?" To this the hunter replied, "If kept always taut, it would lose its spring." The kindly apostle said with a smile, "For the same reason I play with this bird."

We must know how to put occupation aside. In an inaction which is meditative, the wrinkles of the soul are smoothed away.

It is not possible for many to have holidays and vacations at seashores or in mountain glens. We are a busy folk, and we must learn the blessed secret of resting just where we are.

A certain widow lives in one small room on a crowded city street. Four little children are her care: the eldest, a girl of ten years, the youngest, a boy of two. She is the bread earner of the family and is continually busy at her task of washing and ironing. In one corner of her room stands an old rocking chair, and this place is set apart as the family altar. Throughout the day she frequents this, her secret place of prayer, and throwing her large gingham apron over her head, she communes with her Heavenly Father. Her children are taught to be very still at such times. They say one to another, "Mother is talking to God, about us."

A few moments spent in His presence, and she comes forth renewed in body, soul and spirit.

A farmer formed the habit of stopping his plough at the end of every tenth round of the long furrowed field for a few moments of prayer. Not only was his own strength renewed but he gave testimony that his horses did better work and had more endurance because of those moments.

Yes, the worker is far more important to our Lord than the work. To be effective representatives of our Heavenly Father in this day of unparalleled opportunity and challenge, we must assuredly wait upon the Lord and receive from Him life-giving power to live each day in an atmosphere of joyful anticipation—not overwork but overflow.

God will not have us overwork or overstrain,
(Our giant task and puny power, He doth know)
But overcomers by His power obtain,
And by His gracious Spirit overflow.